KV-495-939

NORTHOP COLLEGE
Learning Zone
(01352) 841011

ACCESSION NO. -------------------------------

Please return this BOOK **ON OR BEFORE**
THE LAST DATE STAMPED BELOW.

WELSH COLLEGE OF
HORTICULTURE
LEARNING RESOURCES
CENTRE

British Library Cataloguing in Publication Data
A catalogue record for this book is available from the British Library

ISBN 0.85131.655.7

Published in Great Britain in 1996 by
J. A. Allen and Company Limited,
1 Lower Grosvenor Place,
Buckingham Palace Road,
London, SW1W OEL.

Typeset in Great Britain by Textype Typesetters, Cambridge.
Printed in Great Britain by Hillman Printers (Frome) Ltd, Somerset.

EQUIZ
Advanced

VANESSA BRITTON

J. A. Allen
London

PART 1

Horse management

Care of the competition horse

1 You have a 16.2 hh, eight-year-old, three-quarter Thorough-bred mare that you want to compete in Novice BHS events. Fill in what will be happening during each stage of the yearly programme:

Month/s	Work carried out
January to March	
April to June	
End of June to early July	
Mid to late July	
August to October	
November to December	

2 Most competition horses are stabled. However, this is not ideal as the horse's respiratory system faces problems in the stable environment. Name six of the most common threats to the horse's respiratory system.

1 _____ **2** _____ **3** _____
4 _____ **5** _____ **6** _____

3 The galloping horse produces a temperature rise of 1°C (1.8°F) every five minutes.   true ☐   false ☐

5

4 If your horse finished phase C of a three day event with a temperature of 40°C (103°F) would you carry on to phase D?

a) Yes. As heat is produced during work, this temperature is quite acceptable. ☐

b) No. In order to proceed to phase D the maximum temperature at the end of phase C should be no more than 39°C (102°F). ☐

c) Yes, as long as the horse showed no signs of dehydration and his temperature was not still rising. ☐

5 Which of these studs would you fit to your horse's shoes if:

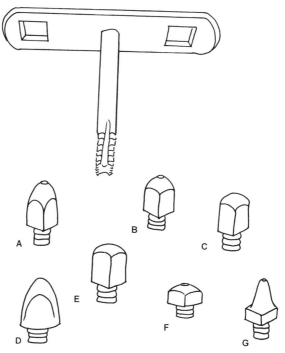

a) The ground was hard. _____

b) The ground was soft. _____

c) You were riding on the roads. _____

6 What is the tap used for?

_____

_____

7 If you are travelling on a long journey with your horse, how frequently should you offer him water?

a) Every two hours. ☐

b) Not at all – horses should not drink while travelling. ☐

c) Just before each feed. ☐

8 Fill in the missing words:

It is essential that you _____ your horse up correctly before a competition. This will ensure that enough _____ is drawn to the _____ that are going to be involved in _____. An insufficient _____ supply results in an inadequate amount of _____ for the _____ muscles, leading to early _____ and the possibility of injury.

9 Name three signs of overstress after a competition.

1 _____ **2** _____ **3** _____

10a What _C_ is happening here between _A_, an untrained muscle and _B_, a trained muscle?

7

b Fill in the missing words: When you train your horse the number of blood _____ in the muscles can multiply by up to _____ % which results in a more efficient _____ supply to the muscles.

The foot, legs and lameness

11 Use the words below to finish these two sentences.

a) The 'insensitive' foot comprises: _____

b) The 'sensitive' foot comprises: _____

the wall	**the coronary band**
the perioplic ring	**the sole**
the frog	**the corium of the foot**
the bars	

12 What is likely to be wrong with your horse if he has a short, choppy stride, he stands over at the knee (when he does not normally do so) and he lifts his front limb up as you approach before you have even touched him?

_____

_____

13 What *O* is degenerative joint disease (DJD) often called?

_____

14 Which is the best definition of the cause of navicular?

a) It is caused by a combination of poor foot conformation and concussive work. ☐

b) It is caused by a deficiency of calcium in the bones. ☐

c) It is caused by galloping too fast for long periods. ☐

15 The diagram shows a simple joint. Fill in the missing words from the sentences below concerning this joint. (Some words are repeated within the sentences.)

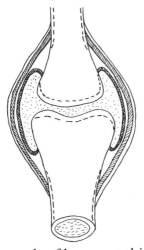

To prevent friction, the ends of bone are shielded with a smooth, but strong substance known as _____. Joints which provide a great deal of movement are lubricated by _____ fluid, which is also known as _____-____. This fluid is contained within a joint capsule known as a _____ which encases the joint. The _____ are lined with _____ membranes which produce and secrete the _____ fluid.

16 Label the diagram using the words you have filled in.

17 The word 'osteitis' means inflammation of the tendon.
true ☐   false ☐

18 What *S* is the term used to describe disease of the hock joint?
S_____

19 A sprain of the plantar ligament of the hock is better known as what?

a) A curb.   ☐

9

b) A thoroughpin. ☐

c) A windgall. ☐

20 On the diagram, shade in on both fore- and hind leg:

a) The suspensory ligament.

b) The extensor muscles and tendons.

c) The flexor muscles and tendons.

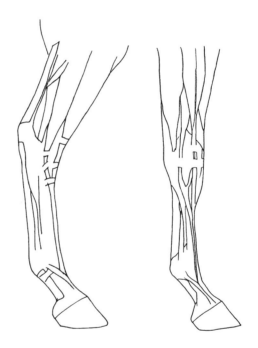

Veterinary procedures

21 Your vet has advised you to apply 'superficial heat' to your horse's limb. How do you do this?

_____

22 Your vet has advised you that your horse needs 'deep heat' treatment. How do you do this?

23 From which vein does the vet obtain blood for a blood test?

a) The aorta. ☐

b) The jugular. ☐

c) The carotid. ☐

24 What *H* is the study of blood? H _____

25 On the diagram, **A**, **B** and **C** show the three distinct healing stages of an incised wound. Give a brief commentary for each stage.

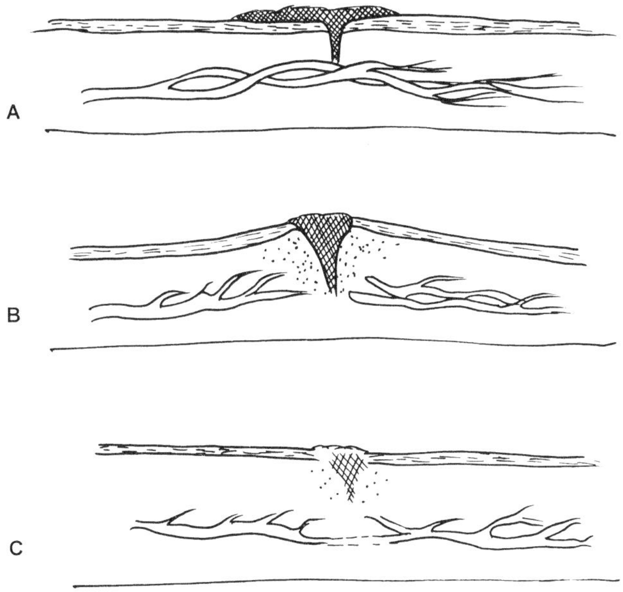

A

B

C

A _____

B _____

C _____

26 Join up the sentences.

a) Nerve blocks

i) is/are used where damage to a bone is suspected.

b) Ultrasound scanning

ii) is/are used for minor surgical procedures.

c) X-rays

iii) is/are used for assessment of tendon and ligament injuries.

27 What must happen to the horse for 12 to 18 hours before a general anaesthetic?

_____

28 If your horse will not stand still while having his eye examined, perhaps because of discomfort from conjunctivitis, what might the vet do?

a) He may put anaesthetic drops into the eye to numb the painful site. ☐

b) He may blindfold the horse. ☐

c) He may use an ophthalmoscope. ☐

29 What does a vet use a fibreoptic endoscope for?

_____

30 What type of shoe is this and what is it often used for?

a) It is a cross or heart bar shoe and is often used to offer relief from laminitis or navicular. ☐

b) It is called a T-shoe and is often used in cases of punctured soles. ☐

c) It is called a three-quarter shoe and is used for corns. ☐

Equine science

31 What is '*materia medica*'?

_____

_____

32 What do the following abbreviations tell you about your vet?

a) BVMS _____

b) BVSc _____

c) MRCVS _____

33 What is the difference between a 'luxation' and a 'subluxation'?

_____

_____

34 What *C* is the type of surgery a vet might use to freeze a wart or sarcoid? C_____

35 The diagram shows an internal view of the horse's heart.

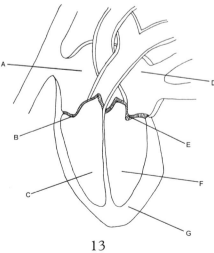

a) Fill in the diagram using the following words:

tricuspid valve   **left atrium**
right atrium   **bicuspid valve**
left ventricle   **right ventricle**
strong muscle of left ventricle

b) Show the paths of:
i) deoxygenated blood with a solid black line;
ii) oxygenated blood with a dashed black line.

36 If your vet said he was going to do a biopsy on your horse, what would he be doing?

a) He would be taking a minute portion of tissue to study in the laboratory. ☐

b) He would be taking samples of blood to study in the laboratory. ☐

c) He would be taking a scraping of skin to study in the laboratory. ☐

37 Join up the sentences.

a) Orthopaedic pertains to   **i)** the eyes.

b) Ophthalmic pertains to   **ii)** the bones and joints.

c) Hepatic pertains to   **iii)** the liver.

38 If a word begins with the letters cardi ... you probably know that the word is going to be something relating to the heart. What subjects do the following beginnings of words relate to?

a) Articul

b) Derm

c) Febr

d) Gastr

e) Neur

39 What *D* is the thin muscular organ that separates the chest cavity from the abdomen? D_____

40 Mark this organ given in question 39 on the diagram and explain what role it plays during exercise.

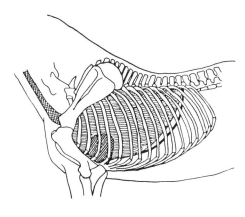

_____

_____

Problem horses

41 What *C* is the name given to dung eating? C_____

42 What is thought to be the most common cause of weaving?

a) Boredom. ☐

b) Stress. ☐

c) Hunger. ☐

43 Crib biting can result in damage to the front teeth.
true ☐   false ☐

44 Explain how you would restrain a horse from getting up while he was lying on the floor. (For example, in order to prevent a cast horse from injuring himself further before he can be turned).

_____

_____

45 What is this piece of equipment called and what is it mainly used for?

_____

_____

46 If you are trying to treat an injury on the near foreleg, yet your horse won't stand still, what do you do?

a) Make the horse lie down. ☐

b) Have someone hold up the other foreleg. ☐

c) Twitch the horse. ☐

47 Explain why twitching works.

_____

_____

48 What is a 'flute-bit' used for?

_____

_____

49 Join up the sentences beginning each with: 'A horse who has a ...'

a) sanguine temperament

b) phlegmatic temperament

c) melancholic temperament

d) choleric temperament

i) is an overreactive type who can often act violently or savagely.

ii) is a timid, easily frightened horse.

iii) is a placid, often lazy, horse.

iv) is a lively, well-balanced horse with a strong character.

50 What type of a temperament do you think this horse has?

The horse's systems

51 What *U* is the system responsible for the disposal of liquid waste from the body? U_____

52 Where does bile come from?

a) The kidneys. ☐

b) The stomach. ☐

c) The liver. ☐

53 Which is which?

a) Food passes into the stomach through the *cardiac/pyloric* sphincter.

b) Food passes out of the stomach through the *cardiac/pyloric* sphincter.

54 The trachea divides into two tubes, one of which goes to each lung. They are called:

a) Bronchi. ☐

b) Alveoli. ☐

c) Bronchioles. ☐

55 The diagram opposite shows the horse's circulatory system. What is the main purpose of this system?

_____

_____

56 Circulation is divided into two parts. What are these parts and what are their functions? Label them on the diagram.

_____

_____

57 Take another look at the diagram.

a) What sites of circulation do A, B, C, D, E and F represent?

A _____ **B** _____
C _____ **D** _____
E _____ **F** _____

b) Shade in the lymphatic system and draw on the diagram where you would find lymph nodes.

c) Label the pulmonary artery, the pulmonary vein, the vena cava and the aorta.

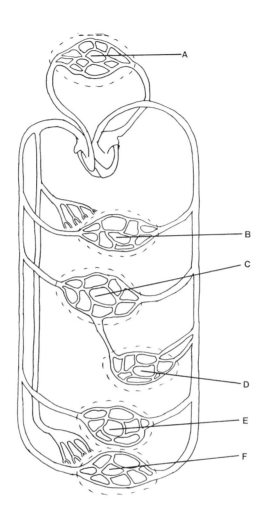

58 What is the skin?

a) It is a circulatory organ. ☐

b) It is a respiratory organ. ☐

c) It is a sensory organ. ☐

59 Fill in the missing words: The skin absorbs _____-_____rays from sunlight. It is then able to make _____ from these rays by a process called _____.

60 Name the lettered parts.

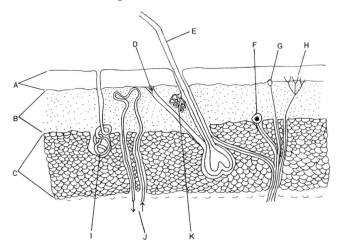

Horse safety and the law

61 Can a horse which weaves be warranted sound?

_____

62 Correct this sentence.
'When leading a horse on foot on a road you should keep to the _left/right_ of the road with _yourself/the_ horse between _the horse/yourself_ and the traffic.

63 What does the term 'loss of use' really mean?

a) That the horse can no longer be ridden. ☐

b) That the horse must be put down. ☐

c) That the horse can no longer be used for the purpose it was bought for. ☐

64 The word 'warranted' on a contract of sale does not guarantee anything but the horse's soundness, unless extra factors are stated afterwards.   true ☐   false ☐

65 What are these two methods of theft prevention?

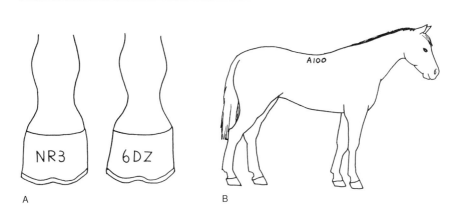

A   B

66 Which of these two methods is a legal requirement for horse ownership?

67 What *M* would arise if you bought a horse on the basis of what the seller told you, or what an advertisement said about a horse, and this information subsequently turned out to be false?

68 If you see a horse with a red ribbon in his tail at a competition, what would this tell you?

a) That it is a young/excitable horse. ☐

b) That it is blind. ☐

c) That it is known to kick. ☐

69 If you failed to slaughter your horse should this be necessary to prevent unnecessary suffering, what act would you be contravening?

70 What does this symbol stand for?

_____

_____

Breeding

71 What *H* is the rubber-like pad often found on the floor after a mare has foaled? H_____

72 To produce a grey foal, the stallion must be a grey.
true ☐   false ☐

73 What percentage of the foal's genetic make-up does the stallion contribute?

a) 25 % ☐   **b)** 50 % ☐   **c)** 75% ☐   **d)** 100% ☐

74 Mares going to stud require a CEM certificate. What does CEM stand for?
C _____ E _____ M _____

75 What type of presentation is this?

a) Breech. ☐   **b)** Dorsal. ☐   **c)** Posterior. ☐

76 Join up the sentences.

a) In the first two-thirds of pregnancy **i)** the foetal growth rate is slow.

b) In the 30 days after conception **ii)** three-quarters of the final birthweight is produced.

c) In the last half of pregnancy **iii)** the spinal cord and brain are developing.

77 A mare's normal oestrus cycle is:

a) 21 days. ☐

b) 28 days. ☐

c) 31 days. ☐

78 What *P* injection brings a mare back into season earlier than usual? P_____

79 What is the result of this injection known as?

a) Short cycling. ☐

b) Early cycling. ☐

c) Quick season. ☐

80 What is this stallion doing?

_____

_____

Nutrition and feeding

81 What is the purpose of adding propionic, sodium propionate and sorbic acid to horse and pony cubes?

a) They preserve the food. ☐

b) They provide extra protein. ☐

c) They make the food more digestible. ☐

82 Correct the sentence.
Hay should be cut *before/after* the seed head *grows/is lost*, when sugar levels in the grass are *high/low*.

83 You have a 15.3 hh gelding, weighing approximately 522 kg (1150 lb), who hacks out every day, is schooled twice a week and competes in showjumping events twice a month. How would you balance his rations as a starting guide?

a) 80–100% hay   0–20% concentrates. ☐

b) 40–50% hay   50–60% concentrates. ☐

c) 60–80% hay   20–40% concentrates. ☐

84 Minerals are added to feed in their salt forms. Do you know which is which? Link the correct terms.

a) Calcium carbonate **i)** common salt

b) Sodium chloride   **ii)** iron

c) Ferrous sulphate **iii)** limestone flour

85 What is the plant on page 25, what are its uses and what is it more commonly known as?

_____

86 What are probiotics?

_____

87 What is the aim of a broad spectrum supplement?

a) To provide a worm-free environment. ☐

b) To provide all of a horse's micro-nutrient needs. ☐

c) To provide minerals which will destroy the gut flora. ☐

88 Correct the sentence. 'The process of *extrusion/extraction* is designed to produce *compound/straight* feeds containing *high/low* levels of digestible *energy/fibre*.'

89 Match the sentences.

a) A horse needs calcium   i) for cartilage formation.

b) A horse needs manganese   ii) for bone growth and devel-
                                      opment.

c) A horse needs potassium   iii) for blood fluid balance.

90 Some of the labels of the parts of the digestive system seem to have become muddled. Can you sort them out?

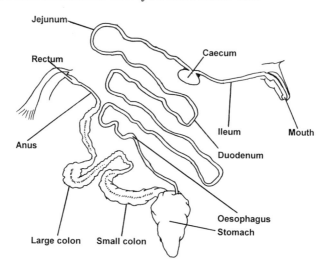

Saddlery

91 Where would you find a skirt, a waist and a seat?

a) On a saddle. ☐

b) On a riding habit. ☐

c) On a pair of women's jodhpurs. ☐

92 Join up the sentences.

a) A Peacock safety iron   **i)** has a forward bulging loop on the outside.

b) A Simplex safety iron   **ii)** has its eye set to the inside.

c) A Kournakoff iron   **iii)** has a rubber band hooked on to the outside.

93 What *L* is the type of girth you would use on a dressage saddle with only two elongated girth straps? L_____

94 What is a Rockwell bridle?

a) A bridle which employs a bit and noseband in combination. ☐

b) A bitless bridle. ☐

c) A bridle used for showing. ☐

95 What is this item of tack used for?

_____

_____

96 What _S_ bit is the Scorrier or Cornish snaffle often called?
S_____

97 What is a 'belly buster.'?

a) It is a girth-tightening device. ☐

b) It is a special type of girth for the horse that always blows out while his girth is being tightened. ☐

c) It is a pad which fixes to the girth to prevent studs from puncturing the belly during jumping. ☐

98 What is the purpose of using a gag as the 'bridoon' part of a double bridle?

_____

_____

99 What _C_ is an 'anti-rearing' bit properly called? C_____

100 What type of martingale is this and what are its advantages over other martingales?

_____

_____

_____

_____

PART 2

Equitation and teaching

Examination of a horse for purchase

101 The standard vetting procedure is divided into five stages. What are these stages (in order)?

1 _____
2 _____
3 _____
4 _____
5 _____

102 How long does the standard vetting procedure take?

a) Less than one hour. ☐

b) One to two hours. ☐

c) A whole morning or afternoon. ☐

103 Which of the following does a standard vetting procedure include:

a) X-rays ☐   **b)** blood tests ☐   **c)** endoscopy ☐

104 Why is a dark loosebox required during the vetting procedure?

a) So that the horse's eyesight can be examined. ☐

b) So that the horse's reaction to dark can be assessed. ☐

c) So that the horse's reaction to bright lights (when turned back on suddenly) can be assessed. ☐

105 Which horse would not be an ideal buy for someone wanting to compete in dressage and why?

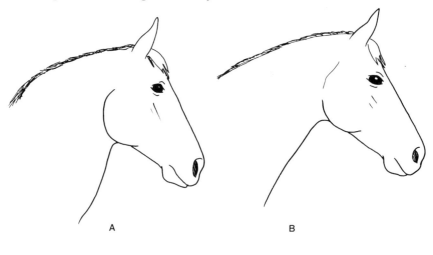

A   B

_____

_____

106 What *S* is a horse that shows signs of abnormality of the nervous system, marked by spasmodic movements of the tail and hind limbs? S_____

107 Which of the following defects/conditions would render a horse 'returnable' if they were not declared at the time of sale.

a) Wind-sucking.

b) A rig at two years or older.

c) Box walking.

d) One that has been operated on for wind trouble.

_____

108 What does the term '*caveat emptor*' mean?

_____

109 When checking the teeth of a horse for purchase the vet will cover six areas. What are these areas?

1 _____ **2** _____
3 _____ **4** _____
5 _____ **6** _____

110 How old is this horse?

a) 6–7. ☐ **b)** 9–10. ☐ **c)** 12–13. ☐

Training the young horse

111 What is meant by the term 'backing'?

a) Riding the horse for the first time. ☐

b) The process of teaching the horse the basic aids. ☐

c) The process in which the horse learns to accept being mounted. ☐

112 Nearly all young horses have difficulty in 'going straight'. Why?

_____

_____

113 What single German word expresses the following description?

'a horse which freely gives all its muscles to use its whole body without any resistance; the horse is supple and unconstrained'. (Reiner Klimke)

a) Takt ☐   **b)** Losgelassenheit ☐   **c)** Schwung ☐

114 If side reins are adjusted too tightly they will shorten a horse's stride.   true ☐   false ☐

115 What is this in-hand training aid called, and why is it often used on young horses?

_____

_____

_____

116 Once a young horse has been backed and is settled with a rider on top, what is the very next thing he must learn?

_____

117 To loosen up a young horse takes approximately:

a) 5–10 minutes.   ☐

b) 15–20 minutes.   ☐

c) No less than 30 minutes.   ☐

118 Cross out the wrong word. As the horse becomes more educated, this warming-up period will *increase/decrease*.

119 Why do we take note of the young horse's tail during a warm-up session?

_____

_____

120 Young horses often buck but which one would worry you more in the young horse if it continued, and why?

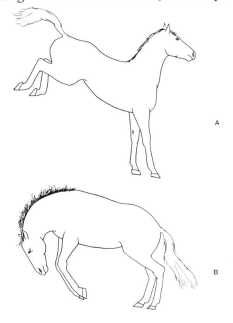

_____

_____

_____

Dressage movements

121 What *P* is a very collected, very elevated and cadenced trot?

P_____

122 From what place in the school is it easiest to introduce full pirouettes?

a) From a circle. ☐

b) From the centre line. ☐

c) Along the short side. ☐

123 Join up the sentences.

a) Rhythm is   **i)** the time it takes for a sequence of footfalls to occur.

b) Tempo is   **ii)** the regular recurrence of a given time interval between one footfall and the next in any of the gaits or paces.

c) Cadence is   **iii)** when a pace or gait has pronounced rhythm.

124 What is the difference between piaffe and passage?

_____

_____

125 What movement is this?

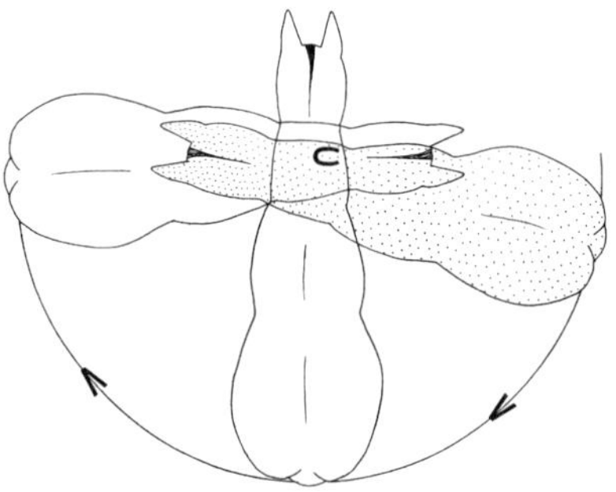

a) Turn on the haunches. ☐

b) Turn on the forehand. ☐

c) The pirouette ☐

34

126 What is the diameter of a volte?

a) 6 m ☐   **b)** 10 m ☐   **c)** 15 m ☐

127 Training a horse to Advanced Level normally takes a period of about five years.   true ☐   false ☐

128 What does 'tempi changes to three-time' mean?

_____

_____

129 If you got a comment on your test sheet that said 'against the hand', what would it mean?

_____

_____

_____

130a) Which shows the correct way to execute a half pass?

A ☐   **B** ☐

130b) Explain what is happening in the incorrect diagram:

_____

_____

Teaching in practice

131 When teaching, what should be your manner?

a) Bold and confident. ☐

b) Soft and endearing. ☐

c) Jolly and loud. ☐

132 How would you overcome the initial fear of most new riders?

a) Laugh and joke from the moment they mount. ☐

b) Allow them to ask any questions they like and answer them in such a way as will not add to their fear. ☐

c) Ensure they are mounted on a schoolmaster who is the correct size for them and aim to encourage familiarity with the horse as soon as possible. ☐

133 What _P_ command should an instructor give in plenty of time before he wants the rider/s to act upon it? P _____

134 What four things should an instructor bear in mind when teaching the canter pirouette?

1 _____

2 _____

3 _____

4 _____

135 What is this movement and how would you ask your pupil to perform it?

_____
_____
_____

136 In what gait is it easiest to teach a rider to lengthen and shorten the stride?

a) Walk. ☐

b) Trot. ☐

c) Canter. ☐

137 When teaching a rider to make smooth transitions, what should he or she be made to realise is all important?

_____
_____

138 What is the maximum length of time a rider should undergo a lungeing session to achieve the most benefit?

a) 10–20 minutes. ☐

b) 20–30 minutes. ☐

c) 30–40 minutes. ☐

139 When introducing a rider to dressage movements, what four aspects should an instructor cover?

1 _____

2 _____

3 _____

4 _____

140 Using the diagram as a visual aid, how would you explain the changing outline to your pupil?

_____

_____

_____

Training in-hand

141 What are the five main objectives of long-reining?

1 _____
2 _____
3 _____
4 _____
5 _____

142 Long-reining can only begin after the horse has been lunged.
true ☐   false ☐

143 When using side-reins during lungeing, should:

a) The inside rein be shorter than the outside rein.　　　☐

b) The outside rein be shorter than the inside rein.　　　☐

c) Both reins be equal.　　　☐

144 If you position yourself slightly behind your horse when
loose-schooling him, what are you encouraging him to do?

_____

_____

145 What *C* is the item of in-hand training equipment seen in the
diagram? _____

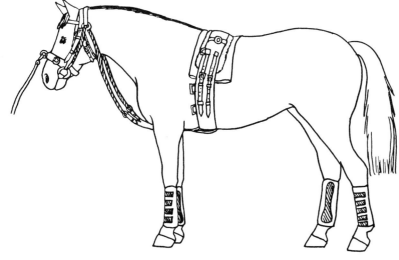

146 Fill in the missing words relating to this item of in-hand training. The _____ is especially useful when a horse has learned to come _____ the bit when lunged in _____-_____. It is also very effective in correcting horses who, because of going in a _____ outline, have built up undesirable muscle on the _____ of their neck. If the horse comes _____ the bit, pressure is exerted on the _____, encouraging him to stretch his head _____. If the horse _____ his head, pressure is again exerted on the _____ and his _____, thus still encouraging him to stretch his whole _____. As soon as he does so, the pressure eases. In this way, a horse soon learns to work in a _____ but _____ outline, adopting a regular and rhythmic gait which is always desirable when lungeing and training horses.

147 Starting a horse (from foal to riding) can be categorised into four separate stages. What are they?:

1 _____

2 _____

3 _____

4 _____

148 Summarise the objectives of in-hand training for the young horse.

_____

_____

149 What *T* is the most important ingredient of each stage of in-hand training? T_____

150 In the diagram we can see the horse working laterally in long reins. The trainer has moved to the right side of the horse in order to work him to the right, but what else should she do to accomplish lateral movement?

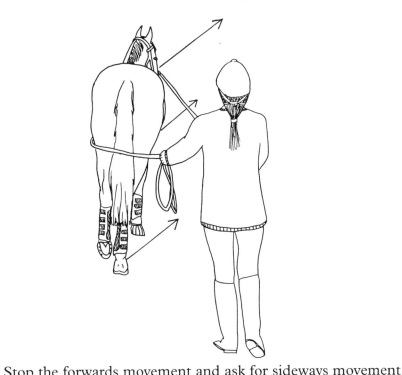

a) Stop the forwards movement and ask for sideways movement by resisting with the left rein and putting pressure on the right rein. ☐

b) Allow forwards movement but also ask for sideways movement by taking a slightly stronger contact on the right rein and giving and taking with the left rein as the horse moves across. ☐

c) Apply an even pressure, pulling to the right with both reins. ☐

Teaching jumping

151 What is the maximum number of pupils you should have in an arena of 20 x 40 m for a jumping lesson?

a) One. ☐　**b)** Six. ☐　**c)** Eight. ☐

41

152 How would you explain the 'sizing up' manoeuvre of a horse before a jump, to a rider who had never jumped before?

_____

_____

153 While energy is imperative for correct jumping, speed is not usually a major element.   true ☐   false ☐

154 What _A_ and _I_ are the components that relate to 'energy under control' which is essential to good jumping?

_____

_____

155 How can this type of jump help a horse to strike off on the correct leading leg in canter after the jump?

_____

_____

156 What lead will this set-up produce?

_____

_____

157 Fill in the missing words.

When jumping, the _____ aim for the rider is to remain _____
and _____ with, and _____ of, the horse while he undergoes
changes in _____, _____ and _____ of _____,thus
making the horse's task as easy as possible.

158 How would you explain 'seeing a stride' to a pupil?

_____

_____

_____

159 What *C* and *T* must a rider be able to ride accurately on the
flat, before attempting to jump? _____

160 Which sentence best describes this rider preparing to land
after a jump?

a) She is too far in front of the movement. ☐

b) She is too far behind the movement. ☐

c) She is well placed for landing. ☐

Competition training

161 What are the four most important physical qualities a show jumping horse should have?

1 _____ 2 _____ 3 _____

4 _____

162 Flat work is very important for good show jumping. If you were to put a good show jumper into a Novice dressage test, what marks should he be capable of scoring for each movement?

a) He should be capable of consistently scoring at least 'sixes'.☐

b) He should be capable of scoring at least two 'eights', and the rest 'fives'. ☐

c) He should be capable of consistently scoring 'eights'. ☐

163 Why is loose-schooling over jumps always beneficial to the jumping horse?

_____

_____

164 Join up the sentences.

a) Cross poles   **i)** encourage/s precise, bigger and rounder strides.

b) A halfway pole between the two elements of a double

     ii) encourage/s a lazy horse to tuck up his forefeet.

c) An A fence   **iii)** help/s to straighten the horse that jumps crookedly.

d) Three trotting poles before the first fence

     iv) encourage/s the horse to jump from trot, which improves co-ordination and activity.

165 What *P* is the dressage movement being taught? _____

166 At what level of competition would you be expected to perform this movement?

_____

_____

167 What is the purpose of placing a pole diagonally across the top of an oxer?

a) It encourages a complacent horse to look more and pay attention to the fence. ☐

b) It encourages the horse to jump higher. ☐

c) If the horse knocks the fence, the pole will roll off, which will frighten the horse and make him more careful next time. ☐

168 When on open land, some fences should be jumped from gallop. Name three such fences:

1 _____ 2 _____ 3 _____

169 What *R* is the French word for collection or, more correctly, 'gathering together'? R_____

170 What is the most important thing to bear in mind when approaching this type of fence?

a) To maintain impulsion at all costs. ☐

b) To approach with a lot of speed so that the horse can reach the top. ☐

c) To approach slowly so that the horse does not trip and stumble. ☐

Competition riding

171 If water is deeper than 46 cm (18 in), at what pace should you travel through it?

a) It would be difficult to do more than a walk through it. ☐

b) It would be difficult to do more than a trot through it. ☐

c) It must be cantered through or the horse will get 'bogged down'. ☐

172 What *O* are flags which must be passed through on the course? O_____

173 At Medium dressage level and for the dressage phase of an FEI senior three-day event, the use of spurs is compulsory.
true ☐   false ☐

174 What speed is required for phases A and C of a three day event?

a) 190 m per minute.   ☐

b) 210 m per minute.   ☐

c) 220 m per minute.   ☐

175 In which types of competition would you expect to see these leg positions?

A

B

C

D

A _____

B _____   **C** _____

D _____

176 Which of the following are classed as a 'resistance' in a dressage test?

a) Napping.

b) Swinging of the tail.

c) Swishing of the tail.

d) Grinding of the teeth.

e) Overtracking.

177 Having entered the dressage arena at A, what should you aim to do in order to keep straight down the centre line?

178 When does a dressage test finish?

a) The moment you salute the judge at G. ☐

b) Not until you have left the arena at A. ☐

c) The halt at G. ☐

179 Why do some course builders often put a style where it has to be jumped out of a corner?

180 Explain what the exercise is on page 49 and say at what level of competition it would be introduced.

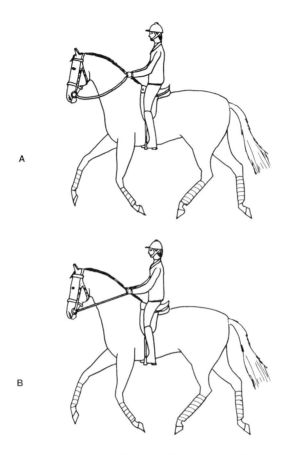

A

B

Dealing with ridden vices and evasions

181 As a horse begins to shy, his paces will become faster.
true ☐   false ☐

182 If a horse is bolting with you, what position should you adopt?

a) Lean forward and go with the movement.   ☐

b) Stay in an upright position with heels down.   ☐

c) Lean back and pull!   ☐

49

183 In order to carry out a buck, a horse must slow down, lower his head and transfer his weight to his forehand. What must the rider do to prevent this from happening and thus avert the buck?

_____

_____

184 There are eight ways in which a horse may try to evade the bit. Can you name these?

1 _____ 2 _____ 3 _____
4 _____ 5 _____ 6 _____
7 _____ 8 _____

185 What is this item of training equipment?

_____

186 Why is it useful for dealing with ridden evasions?

_____

_____

_____

187 What type of shoes are often fitted as a preventive to brushing?

a) Feather-edged shoes. ☐

b) Three-quarter shoes. ☐

c) Fullered shoes. ☐

188 What is the problem if the solution is to turn a horse in a tight circle, keep the head low and maintain forward impulsion?

_____

189 What _N_ is a horse that remains rooted to the spot with forelegs braced, ignoring his rider's wish to go forwards and possibly stepping backwards instead? N_____

190 This bit can be useful in preventing horses from getting their tongues over the bit. What type of bit it is and why does it work?

_____
_____

Riding for the disabled

191 Must a person with disabilities have medical consent to ride?

_____

192 What are the three main sections of riding therapy?

1 _____
2 _____
3 _____

193 What _H_ is the term used to describe a medical treatment method using the horse as a therapeutic intervention.

_____

194 What 'width' of pony is initially needed for a rider with cerebral palsy who has tight muscles inside the thigh?

a) A narrow-backed pony, so that the rider may sit astride comfortably. ☐

b) A wide-backed pony, so that the muscles are encouraged to loosen. ☐

c) A high-withered pony, so that the rider is encouraged to tip backwards. ☐

195 During which activity is this item of equipment used?

a) Vaulting. ☐

b) Driving for the disabled. ☐

c) Handy pony events for disabled riders. ☐

196 In pure leisure riding, the aim is to teach the skills involved in the sport, rather than concentrating on any disabilities.
true ☐   false ☐

197 What is the most important quality provided by a horse to a disabled rider?

a) That of providing mobility. ☐

b) That of providing a sense of direction. ☐

c) That of (perhaps unknowingly) motivating their riders. ☐

198 What are the five absolute contra-indications to riding for a disabled person?

1 _____

2 _____

3 _____

4 _____

5 _____

199 What does ACPRD stand for?

_____

200a) What *L* are these type of reins?

_____

200b) Why are they most often used?

_____

_____

Answers

Part 1   Horse management

Care of the competition horse

1

Month/s	Work carried out
January to March	Fitness work
April to June	Competitions
End of June to early July	Lay-off rest in field/change of scene
Mid to late July	Recovering fitness
August to October	Competitions
November to December	Letting down – roughing off

2 Any from the following:
dust
mould spores
viruses
mites
humidity
bacteria and noxious gases (ammonia from urine-soaked beds etc.)

3 False. It should be every three minutes.

4b) No. In order to proceed to phase **D**, the maximum temperature at the end of phase **C** should be no more than 39°C (102°F).

5 **A**, **D** and **G** for hard ground. **B**, **C** and **E** for soft ground. **F** for road riding.

6 It is used for cleaning the threads and the square holes are fitted over the studs when removing them.

7a) Every two hours.

8 It is essential that you *warm* your horse up correctly before a competition. This will ensure that enough *blood* is drawn to the *muscles* that are going to be involved in *locomotion*. An insufficient *blood* supply results in an inadequate amount of *nutrients* for the *contracting* muscles, leading to early *fatigue* and the possibility of injury.

9 Any from the following:
indications of injury (heat, swelling or pain)
shaking muscles
raised pulse and respiration
reluctance to eat or drink
untypical behaviour

10a) Capillarisation.
b) When you train your horse the number of blood *capillaries* in the muscles can multiply by up to *50%* which results in a more efficient *oxygen* supply to the muscles.

The foot, legs and lameness

11
a) The 'insensitive' foot comprises the wall, the frog, the sole and the bars.
b) The 'sensitive' foot comprises the coronary band, the perioplic ring and the corium of the foot.

12 He is quite likely to have sore shins.

13 Osteoarthritis.

14a) It is caused by a combination of poor foot conformation and concussive work.

15 To prevent friction, the ends of bone are shielded with a smooth, but strong substance known as *cartilage*. Joints which provide a great deal of movement are lubricated by *synovial* fluid, which is also known as *joint-oil*. This fluid is contained within a joint capsule known as a *bursa* which encases the joint. The *bursae* are lined with *synovial* membranes which produce and secrete the *synovial* fluid.

16

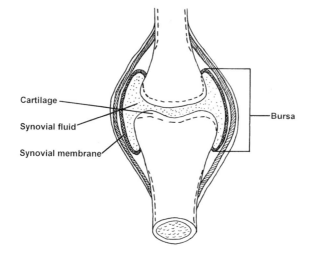

Cartilage

Synovial fluid

Synovial membrane

Bursa

17 False. It means inflammation of the bone.

18 Spavin.

19a) A curb.

20

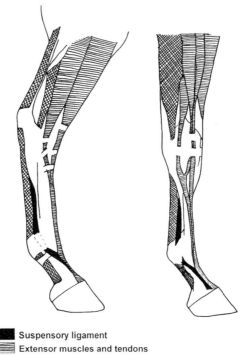

■ Suspensory ligament

▤ Extensor muscles and tendons

▨ Flexor muscles and tendons

Veterinary procedures

21 By using heat lamps, heated pads, hot tubbing or hot poulticing.

22 You should employ the services of a qualified animal therapist who will use ultrasound.

23b) The jugular.

24 Haematology.

25
A As soon as the wound occurs, the skin is broken and the tissues are traumatised. Bleeding then begins.
B The blood vessels swell and exudates then penetrate the wounded site which results in swelling, redness and possibly heat. The resultant swelling serves the purpose of arresting the bleeding and then permits lymphocytes and antibodies (produced by the lymph nodes to fight infection) to resist any infection.
C A scab then forms over the wound and fibrous adhesions are formed. The damaged tissues then slowly return to normal and the blood vessels begin to invade the repaired site.

26 a) + ii); **b)** + iii); **c)** + i).

27 He must be starved.

28a) He may put anaesthetic drops into the eye to numb the painful site.

29 It is used to provide a visual examination of the upper respiratory tract.

30a) It is a cross or heart bar shoe and is often used to offer relief from laminitis or navicular.

Equine science

31 It is a branch of medical science which deals with the source, preparation and use of drugs.

32
a) BVMS = Bachelor of Veterinary Medicine and Surgery.
b) BVSc = Bachelor of Veterinary Science.
c) MRCVS = Member of the Royal College of Veterinary Surgeons.

33 A luxation is a wholly dislocated site (usually referring to a joint), whereas a subluxation is only a partial dislocation.

34 Cryosurgery.

35

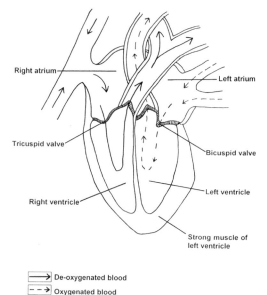

De-oxygenated blood
Oxygenated blood

36a) He would be taking a minute portion of tissue to study in the laboratory.

37 a) + ii); **b)** + i); **c)** + iii).

38
a) articul = joint
b) derm = skin
c) febr = fever
d) gastr = stomach
e) neur = nerve

39 Diaphragm.

40 When travelling at faster speeds the horse's diaphragm adapts its shape in order to increase the size of the lung cavity. This provides extra room for a higher air intake which allows the horse to perform more efficiently at faster paces.

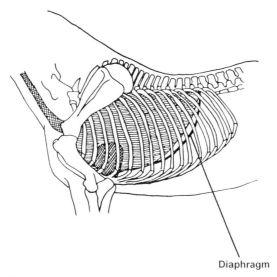

Diaphragm

Problem horses

41 Coprophagia.

42b) Stress.

43 True.

44 Place one knee on the neck just behind the cheekbone. This will prevent him from turning and raising his head – if he cannot do this, he cannot get up!

45 It is called a 'bib muzzle' and is mainly used to prevent horses from tearing their rugs.

46b) Have someone hold up the other foreleg.

47 It is thought that within the muzzle there is an acupuncture point. Once the twitch is applied to the muzzle, the body releases endorphins (the body's own pain-relieving substances) which naturally sedate the horse.

48 It is a bit with holes drilled through it, which is used to prevent wind sucking. When the horse tries to suck air in through his mouth, the wind escapes through these holes and so the 'air swallowing' effect cannot be accomplished.

49 **a)** + iv); **b)** + iii); **c)** + ii); **d)** + i).

50 Melancholic temperament.

The horse's systems

51 Urinary system.

52c) The liver.

53
a) Food passes into the stomach through the *cardiac* sphincter.
b) Food passes out of the stomach through the *pyloric* sphincter.

54a) Bronchi.

55 Its main purpose is to distribute oxygen, water and nutrients throughout the body.

56

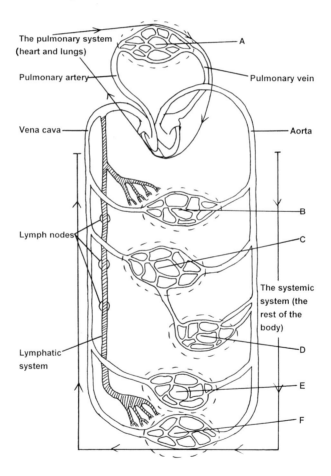

The two parts are the pulmonary system and the systemic system. The pulmonary system is responsible for circulating blood around the heart and lungs. The systemic system is responsible for the circulation of blood around the remainder of the body.

57 **A** = circulation of the lungs
   B = circulation in forelegs, neck and head
   C = circulation through the liver
   D = circulation through stomach and intestines
   E = filtering activity through the kidneys
   F = circulation around hindquarters

58c) It is a sensory organ.

59 The skin absorbs *ultra-violet* rays from sunlight. It is then able to make *vitamin D* from these rays by a process called *synthesis*.

60 **A**   epidermis
   B   dermis
   C   subcutaneous fat
   D   erector muscle
   E   hair
   F   pressure nerve
   G   touch nerve
   H   pain nerve
   I   sweat gland
   J   capillary loop
   K   sebaceous gland

Horse safety and the law

61 No, this is a vice which is considered to be an unsoundness.

62 When leading a horse on foot on a road you should keep to the *left* of the road with *yourself* between *the horse* and the traffic.

63c) That the horse can no longer be used for the purpose it was bought for.

64 True.

65 **A** is called hoof branding; **B** is freeze marking.

66 Neither is as yet a legal requirement of horse ownership.

67 Misrepresentation.

68c) That it is known to kick.

69 The Protection of Animals Act (1911) (England and Wales) and the Protection of Animals Act (1912) (Scotland).

70 It is the British Standards Institute (BSI) 'Kite Mark'. It is an assurance that the item to which it is attached conforms with the current British standard (providing the number also given is a current one).

Breeding

71 Hippomane.

72 False.

73b) 50 %.

74 Contagious equine metritis.

75b) Dorsal.

76 a) + i); **b)** + iii); **c)** + ii).

77a) 21 days.

78 Prostaglandin.

79a) Short cycling.

80 He is displaying Flehmen's posture, which many stallions do in response to an in-season mare.

Nutrition and feeding

81a) They preserve the food.

82 Hay should be cut *before* the seed head is *lost*, when sugar levels in the grass are *high*.

83c) 60–80% hay; 20–40% concentrates.

84 a) + iii); **b)** + i); **c)** + ii).

85 This plant is called comfrey. It is also known as 'knitbone' as it has always been renowned for mending bones. It is a highly nutritious healing and conditioning herb, and valuable as an external application in cases of strain, wounds and tissue damage. It is also said to help arthritis and rheumatism.

86 Probiotics comprise strains of 'live', naturally occurring bacteria which help to re-establish a healthy gut flora after times of stress. They are the opposite of antibiotics.

87b) To provide all of a horse's micronutrient needs.

88 The process of *extrusion* is designed to produce *compound* feeds containing *high* levels of digestible *energy*.

89 a) + ii); **b)** + i); **c)** + iii).

90

Saddlery

91a) On a saddle.

92 a) + iii); **b)** + i); **c)** + ii).

93 Lonsdale girth.

94a) A bridle which employs a bit and noseband in combination.

95 It is called an extending stirrup leather. It is used to lengthen the leather for mounting. Once mounted, it simply hooks back up so that the leather is at the correct length for riding.

96 It is often called a '*stopping*' bit.

97a) It is a girth-tightening device.

98 It gives a greater upward action than a normal bridoon, and thus lifts the head to the desired position so that the curb can ask for flexion.

99 Chifney.

100 This is a Market Harborough. Its advantage over other martingales is that the horse operates it himself. If he lifts his head, a downward pressure is exerted on the bit, but as soon as he lowers his head this pressure is withdrawn. Horses quickly discover this and soon stop lifting their heads above the angle of control.

Part 2   Equitation and teaching

Examination of a horse for purchase

101
1 preliminary examination
2 trotting up in hand
3 strenuous exercise
4 a rest period
5 a second trot-up and examination of the feet

102b) One to two hours.

103 A standard vetting procedure does not include any of these tests and permission must be obtained from the seller of the horse before any such tests can be carried out.

104a) So that the horse's eyesight can be examined.

105 Horse A would not be an ideal candidate for dressage as he has a large jowl and 'thick' glands, which means that there is little room between head and neck, making flexion difficult.

106 A 'shiverer'.

107 All of these conditions would mean a horse could be returned.

108 It means 'let the buyer beware!'

109
1 age
2 alignment
3 abnormal wear
4 sharp edges
5 presence of wolf teeth
6 any abnormalities

110b) 9–10.

Training the young horse

111c) The process in which the horse learns to accept being mounted.

112 Because horses are naturally crooked and have to be taught to go straight by correct training and riding. It is similar to humans having a preference for being left or right handed.

113b) Losgelassenheit.

114 True.

115 This piece of tack is known as a de Gogue. When used in-hand, it is said to be in the independent position. As with most aids, it is passive while the horse is working correctly. It is most beneficial when training young horses as it progresses in a logical way from in-hand to ridden work and is therefore often used throughout a horse's training. From the start the horse has become accustomed to its action and therefore knows the required response. This can directly result in preventing many of the resistances that are commonly seen in poorly trained young horses.

116 He must learn obedience to the forward aids.

117b) 15–20 minutes.

118 As the horse becomes more educated, this warming-up period will *decrease*.

119 Because, initially, it will be clamped down but as the muscles start to relax and so become ready for 'work', it slowly rises and is carried naturally.

120 Horse **B** should worry you more because this is a bronco-type buck which is intended to get you off! Horse **A** is simply full of high spirits and should soon settle once worked.

Dressage movements

121 Passage.

122a) From a circle.

123 a) + ii); **b)** + i); **c)** + iii).

124 In passage the horse moves forwards, whereas in piaffe the horse performs on the spot.

125b) Turn on the forehand.

126a) 6 m.

127 True.

128 It means that the horse changes each leading leg (in canter) at every third stride; for example, a flying change is performed at every third stride.

129 It means that your horse is in opposition to you. Instead of being submissive to your hand, he is resisting or leaning on the bit, which is preventing any impulsion being created from taking him forwards.

130a) B.
130b) In **A**, although the movement has started off correctly, the horse begins to fall out through his inside shoulder which results in him ending up on the wrong bend.

Teaching in practice

131a) Bold and confident.

132c) Ensure they are mounted on a schoolmaster who is the correct size for them and aim to encourage familiarity with the horse as soon as possible.

133 A 'preparatory' command should always be given. For example, 'prepare to trot' should be given just before **H** if the instructor wants the rider/s to trot at **C**.

134
1 The rider should be made aware that it is imperative that he or she maintains a correct, upright and balanced position.

2 That the horse will find the exercise extremely tiring, so it should not be overdone.

3 That the rider will benefit from performing the exercise on a horse that has been well trained and will respond immediately the correct aids are given.

4 The full movement should be built up progressively through quarter- , half- and then three-quarter pirouette, until full pirouette is achieved.

135 The movement is a rein back. You should ask your pupil to take her legs lightly backwards along the horse's side to a point behind the girth where the legs are not applied for any other aid. Then you should ask the rider to put light pressure on to the horse's sides, while at the same time resisting (not pulling) with the reins, thus asking the horse to step backwards. As soon as the movement has been accomplished for a couple of paces, ask your pupil to give with the reins in order that the horse will move forwards a few paces, before halting.

136b) Trot.

137 Preparation is all important – the horse must not anticipate, but the rider must be clear exactly where he or she is going to ask for a transition and give precise and clear aids at that point.

138b) 20–30 minutes.

139
1 What the movements consist of.
2 How to prepare for each movement.
3 How to ride each movement.
4 Overcoming common faults that may be encountered.

140 In this diagram we can see the changing outline from a younger, or untrained, horse's novice outline to a more collected one. This is achieved through methodical, balanced riding, so that the novice horse gradually develops the muscles over his top line, resulting in a more collected outline. Once this has been achieved, the horse will be able to lengthen or shorten his strides within a gait without interrupting his rhythm or tempo.

Training in-hand

141
1 Long-reining builds up the young horse's confidence and trust.
2 It reinforces obedience.

3 It teaches the horse more 'intimate' manners.
4 It builds up the muscles and increases suppleness.
5 It gives the young horse a good mouth before he is ridden.

142 False. Long-reining can be used with a horse that has never been lunged.

143c) Both reins should be equal.

144 You are encouraging him to move forward, or increase the pace, depending on the verbal command also given.

145 Chambon.

146 The *chambon* is especially useful when a horse has learned to come *behind* the bit when lunged in *side-reins*. It is also very effective in correcting horses who, because of going in a *hollow* outline, have built up undesirable muscle on the *underside* of their neck. If the horse comes *behind* the bit, pressure is exerted on the *poll*, encouraging him to stretch his head *downwards*. If the horse *raises* his head, pressure is again exerted on the *poll* and his *mouth*, thus still encouraging him to stretch his whole *top line*. As soon as he does so, the pressure eases. In this way, a horse soon learns to work in a *long* but *rounded* outline, adopting a regular and rhythmic gait which is always desirable when lungeing and training horses.

147
1 Early education, or pre-training from foal to unridden three year old.
2 Training from the ground, in-hand work including loose-schooling, lungeing and long-reining.
3 Backing and riding away.
4 Following-up: elementary training.

148 Through the in-hand training stages, the young horse will learn obedience; he will develop his muscles; will become more supple with an increase in joint flexion, and – because he will learn to engage his hind legs more productively – will show an overall improvement in balance and rhythm.

149 Time is the most important thing. Each horse is an individual and so will progress at a different rate from others. A time limit cannot, therefore, be put on any stage or on any one aspect that is being taught.

150b) Allow forwards movement but also ask for sideways movement by taking a slightly stronger contact on the right rein and giving and taking with the left rein as the horse moves across.

Teaching jumping

151b) Six.

152 You should tell your rider that when the horse approaches a fence he will lower his head and neck in order to work out when he should take off and how he should jump.

153 True.

154 *Activity* and *impulsion* are the two components that are essential to good jumping.

155 By raising the pole on the side you wish the horse to lead, and circling around on the same side, you make the horse aware that he is likely to bang his inside hind leg if he strikes off into canter with it (which he will do if he favours the wrong leading leg when on his less-favourite rein). However, he must approach and take off in trot, and then land and get away in canter.

156 This set-up will encourage a horse to lead with his right hind, which is correct for a left canter lead.

157 When jumping, the *overall* aim for the rider is to remain in *balance* and *harmony* with, and in *control* of, the horse while he undergoes changes in *momentum*, *outline* and *centre* of *gravity*, thus making the horse's task as easy as possible.

158 In order to see a stride during the approach, the rider must evaluate whether their horse's current stride pattern is going to carry him into the take-off zone. If they sense that it is not, then the horse's gait must be extended in order to carry him further forward, or shortened in order to put in another stride. Practising jumping out of a steady, easy rhythm will help the rider to get a feel for this, during which time the horse must be left to judge for himself.

159 *Circles* and *turns*.

160c) She is well placed for landing.

Competition training

161

1 strength

2 suppleness

3 balance

4 co-ordination

162a) He should be capable of consistently scoring at least 'sixes'.

163 Loose-schooling will help the horse to develop his natural rhythm and stride, which allows him to expand his natural jumping technique. As a result, in times of trouble he will be able to revert to his own natural technique and may get both himself and his rider out of difficulty.

164 **a)** + ii); **b)** + i); **c)** + iii); **d)** + iv).

165 Piaffe.

166 At the higher levels of Advanced tests in Great Britain, at Fifth level in the USA and at Intermediare II level and Grand Prix in FEI tests.

167a) It encourages a complacent horse to look more and pay attention to the fence.

168 Any from:
bullfinches
steeplechase fences
stone walls
post and rail fences

169 Rassembler.

170a) Is correct. If impulsion is not maintained, the horse will be physically incapable of continuing to the top of the steps.

Competition riding

171b) It would be difficult to do more than a trot through it.

172 Obligatories.

173 True.

174c) 220 m per minute.

175 **A** general purpose-riding club activities; **B** jumping; **C** endurance; **D** dressage.

176 **a)**, **c)** and **d)** are classed as resistances.

177 Keep the **C** marker between your horse's ears.

178b) Not until you have left the arena at **A**.

179 Because they know that this will very often cause an unbalanced or careless horse to knock it down.

180 The exercise is giving and retaking of the reins. It would be expected in trot and canter during Novice tests in Great Britain and in Training Tests in the USA.

Dealing with ridden vices and evasions

181 False. As the horse begins to shy his paces will become slower, thus alerting the rider to likely problems ahead.

182b) Stay in an upright position with heels down.

183 He or she should bring their body into an upright position with heels firmly down, take a firm contact on the reins to prevent the lowering of the head and drive the horse forwards positively.

184
1 above the bit
2 behind the bit
3 lolling the tongue out of the side of the mouth
4 getting the tongue over the bit
5 leaning on the bit
6 snatching at the bit
7 crossing the jaws
8 opening the mouth

185 This is the de Gogue in the 'command' or 'ridden' position.

186 It is useful for dealing with evasions as it persuades the horse to keep his head within an accepted range of control. While the horse behaves the de Gogue is passive, but should he throw his head about, pressure is applied on the poll and mouth (through the bit), encouraging him to lower his head, and thus bringing him back under control. As this aid can be used during in-hand work, the problem horse should already be familiar with its action.

187a) Feather-edged shoes.

188 The problem is rearing.

189 Nappy.

190 It is called a Fillis snaffle. It works because it is suspended in the mouth, rather than resting on the bars. Thus, when it is adjusted quite high in the mouth there is plenty of room for the tongue, so the horse does not feel the need to put his tongue over it. Additionally, as it is high in the mouth it is very difficult for the horse to get his tongue over the bit.

Riding for the disabled

191 Yes. Medical consent is essential in all cases because the doctor is the person ultimately responsible for the patient's health.

192 1 pure therapy; **2** combined leisure and therapy (which can be subdivided); **3** pure leisure.

193 Hippotherapy.

194a) A narrow-backed pony, so that the rider may sit astride comfortably.

195a) It is a vaulting surcingle.

196 True. In this setting it is ability, not disability, which counts.

197c) That of (perhaps unknowingly) motivating their riders.

198
1 unhealed pressure sores
2 fragile bones
3 haemophilia
4 uncontrolled (by drugs) epilepsy
5 disinclination to ride – after experience

199 The Association of Chartered Physiotherapists in Riding for the Disabled.

200a) Ladder reins.
200b) They are very useful for riders with artificial or severely disabled arm/s.